COLD WAR STEVE PRESENTS...

THE
FESTIVAL
OF BREXIT

 Thames & Hudson

A massive thank you to my favourite photographer – and huge influence – Martin Parr, who very kindly allowed me to use his incredible photographs as backdrops for some of my compositions. Thanks also to John Hinde Images, whose wonderful 1970s photographs of Butlin's provided perfect settings for my notorieties to party like it's 2019. Thanks to Ben (@BeCo74) for *that* picture of Cilla, to Matthew Hamilton, Carl Gosling and Robin Turner, and to Andrew, Sam and Nick at Thames & Hudson.

Finally, a special thank you to my wife, Katy. Notably less annoyed at me being 'on fucking Twitter all the time' now, she has saved my life and helped me more than she could ever realise.

(page 2) Open Mic Night
(opposite) The Opening Ceremony of the Festival of Brexit

First published in the United Kingdom in 2019 by Thames & Hudson Ltd, 181A High Holborn, London WC1V 7QX

Cold War Steve Presents ... The Festival of Brexit © 2019 Thames & Hudson Ltd, London

Illustrations and Captions © 2019 Christopher Spencer

Introduction © 2019 Jon Savage

Alternative Facts – The Cold War Steve story © 2019 Christopher Spencer

British Library Cataloguing-in-Publication Data
A catalogue record for this book is available from the British Library

ISBN 978-0-500-02289-4

Printed and bound in Slovenia by DZS-Grafik d.o.o.

To find out about all our publications, please visit
www.thamesandhudson.com. There you can subscribe to our e-newsletter, browse or download our current catalogue, and buy any titles that are in print.

No Running, Bombing or Heavy Petting

Introduction

BY JON SAVAGE

These images are at once very funny and very cruel. They are designed to be. When organised politics is in chaos – indeed, when politicians are purposely working to harm the population who have elected them – then the only response is a scalding rage which, to avoid its turning inwards, must be transmuted into activism or artistic activity. It's time to send in the satirists, and Cold War Steve is the leading satirist of Benighted Blightonia – the ostentatiously anglophilic breakdown that is Brexit.

Where once it might have been a TV show like *Spitting Image*, or a pop song like the Sex Pistols' 'God Save The Queen' – a timely protest for a previous moment of national delusion – the rules have changed in the 21st century. TV no longer commands a majority viewership; the pop charts are no longer a part of the national conversation. Social media is the new arena, and it's no accident that these images began to appear on Twitter, slowly building a following through their wit and venomous precision.

Britain has gone through the looking glass, as England and Wales drag Scotland and Northern Ireland into their deep nationalistic shadow.

In this Hard Right phase, English politics (as it predominantly is) no longer even pretends to care for most of the population: the Tories are openly punitive, unfeeling and determined to grind the noses of the underprivileged into the dust. No quarter is the game, and none must be given in return in attempts to dismantle this horrific edifice of lying, bullying and childish stupidity. Mockery is a start, but without an edge it is powerless: hence the nightmarish visions of Cold War Steve, a.k.a. Christopher Spencer.

His genius is to precisely pick those targets to be unceremoniously dumped in Shit Britain locations: derelict caravans, roadside fly tips, derelict funfairs, attics scarred by mould, working men's clubs, car boot sales, snow-swept fields and holiday camps, to name but a few – bleak vistas that, like the tower blocks, corrugated iron and brick walls of the late 1970s, appear as a true reflection of a country in the middle of engineered social and psychological impoverishment.

It seems sometimes that Brexit is intent on dragging Britain back, kicking and screaming, to the 1970s – a time of terrible food, casual racism, ideological conflict and street violence. Even so, there was social cohesion. Now there is almost none. This is the reality behind all the talk of 'bespoke deals' and all the other mendacious estate-agent formulations Theresa May and her minions come up with: a degraded environment, below subsistence working wages, the possibility of food shortages. It's time to stock up on tins of Fray Bentos!

By placing the likes of leading Brexit charlatans Jacob Rees-Mogg, Nigel Farage, Theresa May and Boris Johnson in these polluted locations – sitting in a discarded armchair, throwing trainers at a passing tapir and picking up litter (see p. 50) – Spencer removes the trappings of state and tips them straight into the muck that they are creating. They think they're better than the rest of us, but they're not, and stripped of their privilege they look as venal, as cheap and as deceitful as they really are.

To have this effect, Spencer doesn't even have to pick unflattering images – but that doesn't stop him from selecting some choice examples. Page 61 sees a fabulous imagining of a primal woodland scene, with the unpleasantly naked chests of Vladimir Putin, Gregg Wallace, John McCririck and Morrissey disporting behind a permanently bewildered Noel Edmonds. Elsewhere, on page 67, a half-naked Piers

Morgan sleeps it off, while Alan Brazil snores and a blubbery David Cameron runs by in his shorts.

Often, it's an image of some obvious clown in the news, but the cast revolves around a central stock of several characters. These include Donald Trump and Kim Jong-Un – the 'Cold War' – but also repeated tropes like an unflattering picture of Cilla Black, a blowsy shot of a sleeping Alan Brazil, all accompanied by the constant tapir and white dog shit. José Mourinho appears, as do James Corden, Shane Ritchie, Simon Cowell and Cliff Richard – emblems of an unsustaining and unsustainable celebrity culture all.

It's a deliberately nightmarish world. A moralist, Christopher Spencer cuts through the layers of privilege and status to the core of the miasma of Brexit. That this core is not only spiritually and morally corrupt but also physically repulsive is one of his central messages. It's a gallimaufry of fools and knaves, who deserve to be flayed in public. They are quite literally poisoning the world, so it's only fair that there is some comeback.

In every image there is one constant: Steve McFadden, of *EastEnders* fame, whom Spencer typifies as 'watching on with all the existential angst of the everyday man.'* It's telling that he's chosen McFadden's character, Phil Mitchell, a man who has been through hell and back in London's premier soap. In contrast to the North Western warmth and humour of *Coronation Street*, *EastEnders* is often bleak, showing the grim struggle of everyday life in a harsh environment pared down to the bone.

As McFadden wanders through this modern version of a Hieronymus Bosch hell, sometimes accompanied by that other 'everyman' (and fellow *EastEnders* star) Danny Dyer, he remains mute. He is not an agent; he is only a bystander, a witness to the moral and spiritual degradation that austerity and Brexit have unleashed. As Britain spirals ever deeper into disorder, so Spencer's ambition has grown: fairly straightforward montages have developed into huge murals, a state of the nation address.

'It's a bear pit,' Spencer has said about his most ambitious creation, the Liverpool billboard artwork entitled 'the Fourth Estate'. Featuring, among others, Laura Kuenssberg, Simon Cowell, Owen Jones, Steve Bannon, Nick Robinson, Mark Zuckerberg, Rupert Murdoch, Michael Gove, Julian Assange, the Barclay Brothers, Rod Liddle, Paul Dacre, Andrew Neil, Boris Johnson and Rebekah Brooks, this massive collage is 'a circle of hell in which all the odious characters roam'.*

Though by definition newsy and of the moment, there is an urgency to these pictures that goes beyond the demands of current affairs.

Spencer's images speak of a psychological pressure that is both individual – to their creator, expressed in his delight in confronting demons and finding a voice – and collective, providing a visual guide that enables those who are passionately against Brexit to examine what destruction it has wrought at the same as they celebrate its wilful absurdity.

In his sharp moral sense and his ability to create his own complex, detailed worlds, Spencer is the contemporary equivalent of Hogarth or Gillray, both unsparing satirists and social chroniclers. Future social historians will find much beneath the Brexit headlines if they carefully study these works: they will find an anatomy of contemporary England – or, to be specific, one particular part of its anatomy, the arse-end – that might help to explain the delusion that has descended upon the land.

Jon Savage *is a British author, film maker and journalist. His books include* Teenage: the Creation of Youth 1975–1945, 1966: The Year The Decade Exploded, *and the award winning* England's Dreaming: Sex Pistols and Punk Rock *– now regarded as the definitive history of British Punk in the late 1970s.*

* Nazia Parveen, 'Brexit visions of "Cold War Steve" showcased on Liverpool billboard'. *Guardian*, 30 November 2017

Turf Accountants

Café Brexit

Festival of Brexit – Zone One

Jubilations

The Adequate-Food Man

Works Holiday 2019 – Part One

Festival of Brexit – The Flyover Zone

Portacabin Revelry

Bank Holiday Pie Rolling

Here Comes the Tinned Pie Man – Part One

(*opposite*) Untitled

Here Comes the Tinned Pie Man – Part Two

Works Holiday 2019 – Part Two

The Lay-by

Platinum Jubilee Celebrations, 2022

Detritus

Festival of Brexit – Zone Three

Envoys

The Club – Part One

Brit Awards 2020

Loungers

The Club – Part Two

The Club – Part Three

Pub

Domino Night (the Doms)

The People Who Live in the Attic

Diner

Meat

Angling

Dance

Adequate Food

Stockpile

Judges' House

ds' Night

Throwing Lonsdales

right Vacuums

Bootiful

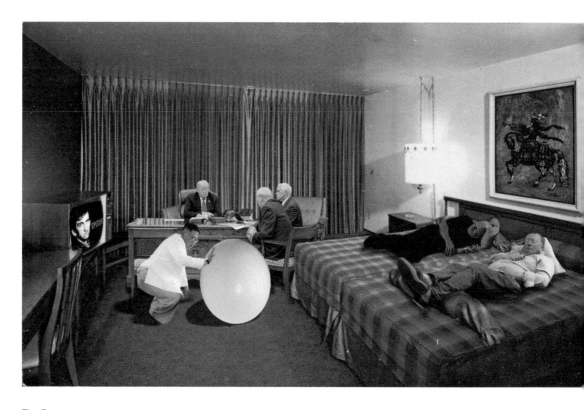

The Egg

Night of the Big Trousers

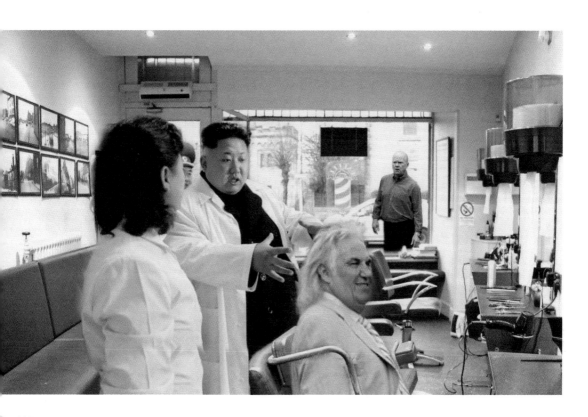

Man Hair

Untitled

ascal

The Coppice

The Flat

63

Community Centre

Pontiff Going to the Outdoors

The Woods – Part One

(opposite) Hot in the City

Three Lions

Captain Beaky

The Best Man's Speech

The Royal Couple's First Public Engagement

The All-Dayers

No Paperwork Required

Pensive

Carbooters

The Buffet

House Meeting

(*previous*) The Potato Pickers 2020

Carnival Day

Christmas Future – Part One

The Woods – Part Two

Last of the Summer Cunt

(opposite) Shoefayre

Waiting for the Coach Driver

(*opposite*) Untitled

Locals

(*opposite*) 11pm, March 29th 2019

Untitled

The Wake

Holiday 2020 – Part One

Holiday 2020 – Part Two

Holiday 2020 – Part Three

Flat-Roof Pubs and Tinned Pies

Hotel Room

Live Turn

Mr Egg

Savoury Pies

Hot Tubs

Guests

Global Britain

The I I c

State Funeral

Rehab

The Yates' Wine Lodge

Welcome

(opposite) Flytipping

Best Buys

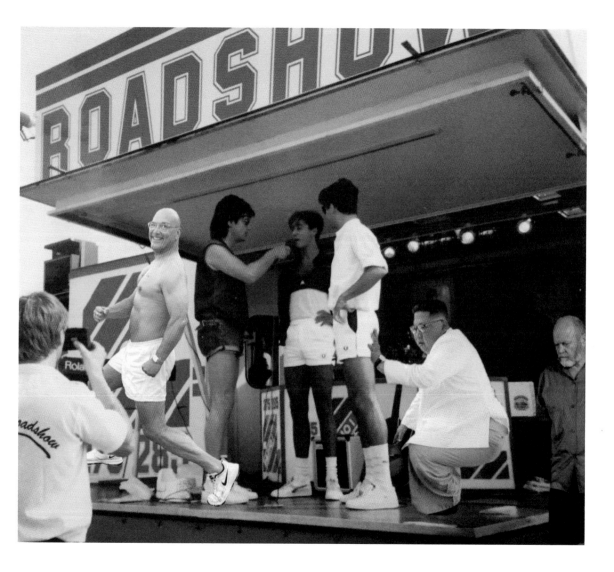

Artical 50 Night

(*previous, left*) High Street

(*previous, right*) Roadshow

War Games

Preparations Are Underway
for the State Visit

G9 Summit

(opposite) Public Convenience

The Pub Car Park Fight

(*opposite*) Christmas Future – Part Two

Sunlit Uplands

The Glade

Universal Credit

(*opposite*) The Fourth Estate

Holiday 2020 – Part Four

The Night Bus

Shoe Shopping

Salon

Cooked Meats

Look At What You Could Have Won

Tinned Hams

Gornal and Sedgley Bowls Team, on Their Way to Cradley Heath Libs for an Away Match

Nativity

(*overleaf*) Noel Edmonds in the Woods

137

Alternative Facts – The Cold War Steve story

BY CHRISTOPHER SPENCER

I was born in Solihull hospital in April 1975, and had a fairly unremarkable childhood in a Birmingham suburb. Dad worked at a British Leyland car plant in Longbridge. Mom didn't work, but when my two younger brothers and I were a bit older she went to college and eventually became an English teacher.

Although I didn't appreciate it at the time, both my parents were hugely influential in what I'm doing now. Both were Socialists (I have a very early memory of my mom ripping up a Tory leaflet that came through the door), so I couldn't understand why my best friend's dad loved Margaret Thatcher so much – 'but she's an evil baddie,' I'd say to my friend, who would just shrug his shoulders as we carried on playing on the corrugated roofs of nearby garages.

One of the biggest influences was their taste in television programmes. I remember the big wooden TV had separate buttons for each of the – then just four – channels, each of which had a green bit of plastic indicating which channel had been selected. On buttons two and four the green had completely faded away, while number three (ITV) remained forever a luminous, bright green. I still don't think I ever watch ITV. Instead, we would watch brilliant programmes like *The Young Ones*, *Arena* (I can't imagine any of my daughters sitting through an episode of *Arena* now…), *The Tube*, *In At The Deep End* and *Fry and Laurie*.

Art had also always been a passion of mine. I remember being completely fascinated by the paintings in my mom's art books, and I was constantly drawing – forever taking out the inside of felt tips to try and eke out a bit more colour – spending countless hours making my own comics (which my mom still has!). All of which meant that I decided to enroll at an art college after finishing my GCSEs.

Though I completed college, things started to drift after a rather lacklustre attempt to get onto a Fine Art degree course at Wolverhampton University ended in rejection (the portfolio of work I'd presented consisted entirely of paintings of winklepicker shoes). I ended up forming a band called Whelk, certain that we were going to be huge. I came up with what I thought to be amazing song titles and focused heavily on image – forgoing actual songwriting and band practice.

I started full time work in 1994 in various factories and warehouses, and became an alcoholic at around that time. I'd been suffering with depression since my late teens, and my discovery that booze took away my anxieties was a revelation. I continued to struggle with my mental health for years, self-medicating with drink and drugs, an exercise culminating in a complete breakdown and suicide attempt in January 2016.

After a period of time in hospital, I began to make collages on my phone – very crude at first, just putting Noel Edmonds's hair on other celebrities. I shared these on Twitter, and the positive response I got was really uplifting. I then had the idea to superimpose Steve McFadden (a.k.a. Phil Mitchell) into Cold War scenes. I'm still not entirely sure how or why I came up with that. I've not watched EastEnders since the late '80s, but found the photos of 'drunk Phil' or 'Phil on crack' quite alluring. The Cold War, and more

specifically the history of the Soviet Union, has always interested me, and I'd recently read Simon Sebag Montefiore's brilliant books on Stalin (Young Stalin and The Court of the Red Tsar).

The moment I placed Phil Mitchell – bottle of Scotch in one hand, aggressively pointing with the other – next to Leonid Brezhnev and the rest of the Politburo, watching a May Day parade from the Kremlin balcony, I knew I'd hit upon something with great potential. I set up a new Twitter page to share these 'Phil Mitchell in the Cold War' scenes, and it quickly took off. Making the images became a superb coping mechanism for me, and definitely helped my recovery and ongoing maintenance.

Since then, the Twitter account has evolved. It had to; it was essentially one joke: the incongruity of Phil Mitchell with Reagan, Gorbachev, etc., so I started to involve other 'celebs' and scenarios. This was met with a Dylan-going-electric type backlash at first, with Cold War Steve purists demanding the return of the stripped-back acoustic numbers. Fuck that. I was enjoying it too much, my mental health was the most stable it had been for years, I'd been drink and drug free for over a year and, most pertinently, there was Brexit…

This catastrophic event would have most certainly led to a relapse for me, but I channeled my anger and horror into my compositions. Rather than getting pissed, hoofing a load of cocaine and ranting, I composed pictures; pictures that on the face of it are amusing tableaus of incongruity, but which actually, I hope, show up the despicable, lying, sociopathic cunts for what they are. I have often been remonstrated for using the 'post plane crash' photo of Farage, or pictures of Fred West, being told that it was in 'poor taste'. My response was, and still is, that my using a picture of a bloodied, post-plane crash Farage is nowhere near in as bad taste as Farage himself, or the hateful, bovine bigotry that he shits out of his massive, amphibian mouth.

I consider my work to be comedy, political satire and art. I think first and foremost it is comedy – not all of my images are political or especially arty, but I always try and make them funny. As the subject matter has evolved, so has my style of working. I still compose my 'photomontages' on my phone, but the apps I use – which are still cheap App Store ones – have improved, and since my first exhibition (at The Social in London) I've become much more aware of things like image resolution.

I now start a composition by purchasing a high-resolution background image, before adding my subjects via the Pixomatic app. That said, I am not a 'Photoshopper'. I've had 'Photoshoppers' remark on my 'shit photoshops' – 'the tones of the faces are wrong,' 'the shadows are shit,' and what have you. The fact that I make them on my phone, often on the bus to work, is crucial to what I do. If I spent hours on them, Photoshopping for ages to make them look impeccable, they would lose all of their spontaneity and their DIY ethos.

That said, technological advances have enabled me to try to emulate the expansive, often bleak and dystopian scenes, replete with fantastical sub stories being played out by grotesque characters, of my major artistic influences: Bruegel and Bosch. Like them, I use a lot of symbolism in my pieces, which people can interpret if they so choose. The tapir (Lucky Ian), for instance, is a symbol of hope and diversity, the Lonsdale slip-on trainer a symbol of Brexit and the much used Frey Bentos pie references both the notion of 'adequate food stockpiling' and Brexiteers' desire to go back to a time when there was no diversity on Britain's high streets – a time of tinned pies, corned beef, potatoes… insipid, bland, shit, but Brrritish! The white dog shit is also a reference to that Brexit mindset – bring back white dog shit… and the Mini Metro.

I am flattered to even be mentioned in the same breath as artists like Bruegel, Bosch, Gillray and Hogarth, but I don't feel I deserve to be. However, it is a fertile time for the type of satirical work that I do – Gillray had his grotesque characters (The Prince Regent, Napoleon) and I have mine (Kim Jong-un, Trump, Boris, etc.). I do have an increasing cast of regulars, from politicians and despots to z-list celebrities and corpulent ex-footballers. They share equal footing as the lines of their power and influence become ever more blurred.

The thing I enjoy most from all of this is the feedback from my followers. Their comments are always hilarious and enhance the original post immeasurably. I feel like we are a massive club of like-minded people – compassionate, liberal and aghast at world events (Brexit, Trump, the rise of bigotry and fascism). We are together in being scared by what's happening, but at the same time laughing at these fucking absurd idiots who are responsible. We will win.